Let me
Express
my
Feelings

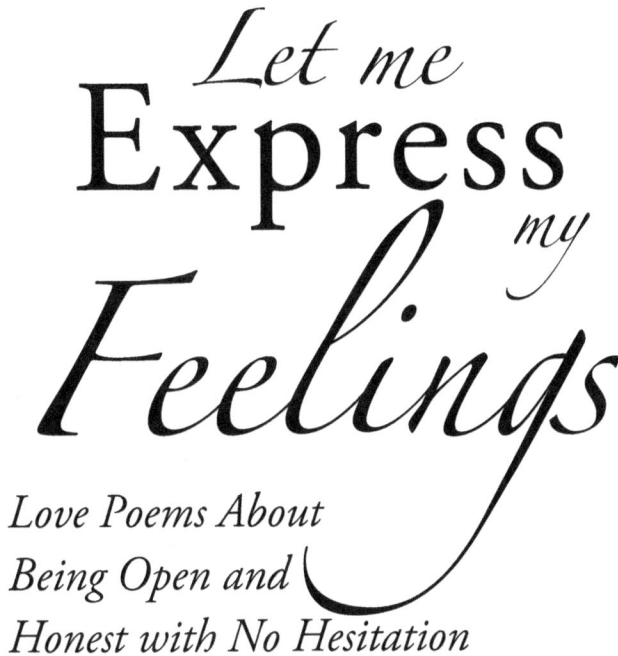

Let me Express my Feelings

Love Poems About Being Open and Honest with No Hesitation

Freddie Moore

LET ME EXPRESS MY FEELINGS: LOVE POEMS ABOUT BEING OPEN AND HONEST WITH NO HESITATION

This book is written to provide information and motivation to readers. Its purpose is not to render any type of psychological, legal, or professional advice of any kind. The content is the sole opinion and expression of the author, and not necessarily that of the publisher.

Copyright © 2020 by Freddie Moore

All rights reserved. No part of this book may be reproduced, transmitted, or distributed in any form by any means, including, but not limited to, recording, photocopying, or taking screenshots of parts of the book, without prior written permission from the author or the publisher. Brief quotations for noncommercial purposes, such as book reviews, permitted by Fair Use of the U.S. Copyright Law, are allowed without written permissions, as long as such quotations do not cause damage to the book's commercial value. For permissions, write to the publisher, whose address is stated below.

Printed in the United States of America.

ISBN   978-1-951913-56-4   (Paperback)
ISBN   978-1-951913-57-1   (Digital)

Lettra Press books may be ordered through booksellers or by contacting:

Lettra Press LLC
30 N Gould St. Suite 4753
Sheridan, WY 82801, USA
1 303-586-1431 | info@lettrapress.com
www.lettrapress.com

Thank You

I would first like to thank God for blessing me with the life that I'm living, because without him being in my life nothing would be possible. I would like to dedicate this to my late father, and to thank God for giving me time to tell him that I loved him. To my mother to whom I love with all of my heart, to my grandmother because she taught me a lot growing up as a child. To my high school teachers Mrs. Terry, Mrs. Lewey, Mrs. Jones, Coach Larry Peck, my high school football coach, the late Coach W.L. Burns, and last but not least, Mrs. Ernestine Robinson, I would like to thank her for the lessons and for the realities that she taught me. She taught me to always be a proud black man and to stand up for what I believed in. I would like to say thank you and I love you to all of the people that made a difference in my life.

Contents

To my first love 1
Love, Lust, Temptation 4
Somebody Else's Girl 7
Looking for Love..9
Letting Go of Our Ego 11
Enough is enough 13
My Promise... 15
My Love.. 16
Love Is 17
I Feel For You... 18
My Heart to Yours 19
Dreams of You 20
Open Your Heart 21
Finding Love...22
My Heart Glows 23
Trusting 24
The List 25
To You 26
My Heart 27
You Will Never Be Alone 28
You Touch My Soul..29
Time After Time 30
My Desire 31
Love Makes Us...32
The Things I Feel..33
Things of the Heart 34
My First Love..35

Being in Love with You 36
Forever More 37
Take My Hand 38
Dreams 39
Falling in Love 40
I'm sorry 41
Your Heartbeat 42
Love is Pure 43
Give Me a Chance 44
Loving You is Easy 45
Your Lover, Your Friend 46
My Lover, My Friend 47
Ask Yourself 48
Thoughts of Loving You 49
The Passion 50
Your Eyes 51
Forever Yours 52
Your Beauty 53
Thinking of You 54
It's Only Natural 55
A Man's Love 56
Your Inner Beauty 57
Teach Me 58
My Greatest Vision 59
It's Real 60
Reason to Believe 61
In My Heart 62
A Life Together 63
Shower You With Love 64
To Be Your Man 65
Statue in My Heart 66
My Plan 67
Making Love to You 68
Worth the Wait 69

Sweetest Song...70
Trust Me 71
Special Love 72
A New Love 73
Love is Blind 74
Life is Love...75
Trust in Me...76
On My Mind 77
Do you Think of Me..78
Till the End..79
Love For a Year..80
Trust Me Again..81
Moments in My Life 82
Second Chance...83
Without You 84
Dreams of You 85
Touch From You 86
I Love You...87
Hands of Time...88
Chance on Love 89
Caring Ways 90
What's Love 91
Together...92
Time to Grow 93
Give Me a Chance..94
Will You Forgive 95
I Miss You..96
You Are 97
I Will Never Tire..99
You're on my mind 100
A Broken Heart.. 101
Imagination..102
My Choice 103
A Love Like Mine 104

Within You 105
Listen to Your Heart.. 106
Living Without You... 107
Broken Heart 108
I Remember 109
I Wonder.. 110
My Lover 111
Outside Looking In.. 112
A Lonely Man 113
My Mistake.. 115
The Love is Gone 116

To my first love
To my love
And to the one I desired to love

There are things in the world that we need to survive. We need food to eat, air to breathe, and water to drink. Those are three basic needs that we need to survive, but getting to much of what we need can kill us, eating to much will kill us, if we get to much air we can't breathe and getting to much water we will drown.

There is one thing that I know we can't get enough of and that's love. Getting to much love will not kill us, but not getting enough will kill the heart. We will never understand what love is, we can't smell it, we can't taste it and we can't see it. We can see the affects that love has on us. We don't have to have a sense of taste or sight; we should feel blessed, because the heart doesn't need it.

The heart is the only organ in the body that has control over our mind and body. The heart is the central nervous system. Believe it or not it controls everything. I sometime wonder how one organ has the power to control every emotion that we have. We all know that time is the only thing that will heal a broken heart. We all have heard the saying that love makes the world go round, but if we look at it our bodies are the world and our heart is in each and every one of us.

Love is no different than anything else. What I mean is, love something that has to be taught. Some of us don't know how to love, because we haven't been taught how to love.

Growing up as a child in my family my parents taught us a lot of things, but love was not one of them. Growing up as a child I can honestly say that I never heard that word in my home.

I never once heard my father tell my mother that he loved her and I never heard her say it to my father. We knew our parents loved us, but we never heard them say it to us and we didn't say it to them.

Let me back up for a minute, about my father telling us that he loved us. The few time that my father told us that he loved us is when he was intoxicated.

Some people say that we get drunk to speak our sober thoughts. I'm not putting my father down, but that's just how it was. It was hard for him to say it to us I believe, because he was not told that as a child. And the first time my mother said it was when John, my oldest brother went into the military. I remember him calling home and after every phone conversation, she would end by saying Momma loves you. To this day my brothers and sisters are not saying it enough to one another. When John and my other brother Guy write letters to me, they always end by telling me that they love me. There was one particular girl that I was dating and they said it to each other all the time. I mean to me it was strange to hear those words. Her mother would be talking to her older sister on the phone and at the end of every conversation her mother would say" I love you." That sounded weird to me, the first thought that popped into my mind was that black people don't do that because I never grew up in my family hearing that.

Like I said I'm not saying that the love wasn't there, it just wasn't expressed verbally enough. Being around family you could see the love that they had for one another. Like I said earlier she was the love of my life and you will never get over your first love. She taught me a lot about how it felt to be loved and how it was to love. Love was a seed that she planted in my heart, and she nourished it to make it grow. I must say that my heart was broken when we parted ways; I thank God for the things that she brought out of my soul. To this day I still think of her, and I would sometime wonder if she ever thought of me, during our absence. I really believe that my life has become a full circle. I've loved, I've been loved and now I'm expressing my love. I have been travelling in a straight line all my life like most of us. Trying to find our purpose in life we continue on a straight path. In order to complete our circle we must be happy with what we have done and what we haven't done. I can honestly say that my circle is complete, and it is up to all of us to complete our own circle. I hope the words that you read will reach your mind, heart, and soul. Thank you, and God will forever bless you.

Love, Lust, Temptation

Those three words have been around since the beginning of time; better yet those three actions have been around as well. They were here before we were born and they will be here long after we are gone. But we all sometimes act as if we have discovered something new, but we haven't. I believe that love, lust and temptation started at the beginning of mankind in the Garden of Eden with Adam and Eve. God made Adam, and he had dominion over everything. God saw that Adam was still lonely so he made Eve along with temptation. You see God told Adam and Eve they could eat from any tree in the garden of Eden except the tree of life. Over a period of time they became curious about the tree of life. Eve began to temp Adam about eating the forbidden fruit. After a while Adam fell into his temptation. And we all know what happened after that. One thing that I do know is that was the power of a woman that she has over a man.

Next I would like to talk about Samson and Delilah, we all know the story about Samson and Delilah, if not read the book. God had blessed Samson with unimaginable strength and the strength would lie in his hair. That secret only God, Samson and his mother shared. Samson fell in love with a woman named Delilah.

Delilah did not love Samson she only had evil intentions toward him. She asked Samson three times were his strength lie and three times he lied to her. Samson loved Delilah so much that he finally told her that his strength lies in his hair, and if he would cut it he would become a normal man.

If, a woman can convince a man to tell her a secret that is between him and God the thing we call love is powerful. In today's age we might call it whip appeal. Now, we come to lust, which is the strongest of all.

There is a story in the Bible about this King that saw a beautiful woman bathing. After seeing her he just had to have her. They met and had a romantic relationship and she became with child. This woman was also a married woman and her husband was away at war. When the King found out that the woman he had slept with was with child, he sent for her husband to come home. He wanted him to lay with his wife, so that he would think he was the father of this child that she was carrying. The husband refused to do so stating that he would not feel right knowing that men were dying in battle while he was getting pleasure from his wife. The king than sent him back to battle and gave instruction to place him on the frontline were fighting was most dangerous and so that he would be killed.

It just so, happened that the man was killed. The lust of a King and this man wife caused this man to die. If I ever meet a woman named Eve, Delilah, or Basheeba I'm going to run in the other direction.

Love, Lust and Temptation we can only control them as best we can.

Being faithful will help us out a lot when it comes to lust and temptation.

Sometimes we think that the grass is greener on the other side. That is until we get to the other side.

If you are in a relationship, I don't care if you are male or female, white, black, red, yellow or brown being unfaithful is the hardest thing to get past. Some people think that they are to smart or so smooth that they can't get caught. I don't care who you are if you keep being unfaithful eventually you will get caught. Like my grandmother would say you will reap what you sow.

Speaking from a man's point of view, we don't know when enough is enough. For example, if our lady catches us it's over for us. The first thought that we are going to get is that I did it to her now she's going to do it to me.

Ladies you don't have to do a thing, all you have to do is just make us think you are doing something. Ladies I hope this doesn't get me in trouble, but if you catch your man cheating this is what you should do. Whatever time you get off work show up about forty-five minutes later, if you have a cell phone when he calls don't answer or turn it off.

Believe me if he loves you he will think twice about doing it again. The thing that will hurt the most of us men today is to find out that their lady can be touched by another man. It does not have to be a physical touch with hands; I'm talking about mentally touching her. You see if her mind can be altered you can than plant a seed of thought, and the hardest thing for a man to get over is to know that his lady is thinking about another man. It's the same way with men, if a woman's touches our mind we began to wonder what it would be like to be with that woman. If your man or ladies don't do anything about it that seed will continue to grow and that's when we want to fulfil our curiosity to see what the other person has to offer. Sometimes our mind can take us places that our physical body will never go, but on the other hand our mind can take us to where we want to be. I suggest that we should plant our seed ourselves and that way his/her mind will not have room for someone else's seed.

Somebody Else's Girl

As men we all have had someone else's girl. What I mean by that is being with a woman that is in a relationship with another person. In the old days they probably would have said a" woman that belongs to another man". To me that sounds barbaric, because no person can own another. Slavery was abolished a long time ago. Some of us choose to do that because we are lonely, other does it because we don't want to take on all of the obligations of being in a relationship. We want to be the one that hit and run.

Being with someone else's lady can be a stressful situation, always having to look over your shoulders, getting nervous every time you hear a knock at the door or whenever the phone rings. You know the cemetery is full of men that took a chance on being with someone else's woman. There you are laying six feet under and someone else is going to pick up where you left off. There will come a point and time in our lives when we are going to want our own women. It's okay to share a lot of things in our lives but a woman is not one of them. A woman should be held at the highest regard, and we men should worship the ground in which they walk, because our lives started with them.

Ladies if you are reading this I'm not telling you what I think you want to hear, I'm telling you how I feel. Don't get it wrong but there are a few women out there doing the same thing. They would rather have someone else's man rather than getting their own. I'm not trying to call anyone out but the truth is the truth. Sometimes I often ask myself the question of who's doing it more. But that's a question that we will never know the answer to. Just remember if you are a man and you are involved with another man's woman, or if you are a woman that is involved with another woman's man, don't be the pot that's trying to call the kettle black.

The thing is we men cannot stand the thought of another man touching our ladies. It is something that is so hard to explain. I don't care who you are. The thought of another man touching your wife or girlfriend will literally make you want to kill somebody. Say for instance if we are married and we have a girlfriend on the side, if that girlfriend stepped out on you, it wouldn't bother some of us that much. But if our wives did that same thing you would want to take his life and hers too. To make a long story short if you can't take it, don't dish it out.

Looking for Love

I think that love is one thing in life that we should all experience. It is also something in life that we will never understand.

When it's good it's good, but when it's bad it hurts. We will never understand how can something that feels so good hurt so bad.

We all enter into relationships with good intensions, but along the way our actions change. We are the one's that change, but love will always stay the same. We sometimes think that when we find love in a relationship that the work stops there, but we are wrong, that's where the work begins.

You should look at it like this, if you go to a car lot and buy a car in order for you to keep that car; you are going to have to work to pay for it. And when you are living in that house, you are going to have a few bills, like the utilities, phone, cable, and Internet. If, you do not work to keep them on we all know what's going to happen, you will lose it all. That's the same thing that will happen in a relationship. If you do not continue to work on it, it will end. When meeting someone new, we always put our best foot forward. But when we have gotten what we were after, we relax. That is the biggest mistake we could ever make. Why? Because, if a sprinter is in the one hundred yard dash, he does not relax if the other runners are behind him.

He keeps the same pace until he crosses the finish line, because he knows that as soon as he relaxes someone else is going to win the prize.

We must always remember that someone else wants our prize as much as we do and will do whatever it takes to get it, because whatever we don't do someone else will, and they will probably do it better than we did. If you are in a relationship, be in it to win, just because you have the prize now does not mean that the race is over.

Letting Go of Our Ego

Thorndike Barnhart dictionary gives the definition of ego,

1) The individual as a whole with the capacity to think, feel, and act; self.
2) Sense of worth; self-esteem.
3) Conceit; self-importance.

I like the last definition the most, because men some of us are walking around and can't nobody tell us nothing. Why? Because, we all have (the big head).

Being in a relationship, is the wrong place to have an ego, because that could lead to a lot of things like jealousy, content, and hatred.

I have heard some cases where men didn't like it if their spouses make more money than they did or lived in a better house or drove a nicer car. Having an ego can be a dangerous thing in a relationship.

As men we sometimes think that we always have to be on top. You see if our spouses make more money than we do, some of us would feel like we were beneath them.

To be honest the only time we want our women to be on top and us men beneath them is in the bedroom. That is really the only place some of us wants to give our women control. Just because we are not on top all of the time does not mean that we are less of man. We need strong women in our lives; a strong woman will lift us up when we are down. Sometimes pride may get in the way, because some of us are ashamed to ask our ladies for help. A strong woman will stick by you when you are up or down, she will help you only if you are willing to help yourself.

No woman wants a man who would prefer to drown in her own self-pity. Before she will help you, you must first want to help yourself, because no one wants to carry dead weight.

The biggest problem that most of us men have is that we try to keep the things that are bothering us to ourselves. That is the wrong thing to do, because all that it does is push our women farther and farther away.

I know, because it has happened to me. We should be more open about our feelings and stop thinking that by doing it will make us look weak. One of the strongest men in the world is a man that will ask for help. It doesn't matter if it's your wife, girlfriend or best friend, be a man and ask for a hand.

Enough is enough

As I sat down to write about my last topic, it was kind of hard to find a place to start. Some of us have been in situation when we didn't want to accept the fact when enough is enough. We sometimes try to hold on to a marriage, boyfriend or girlfriend hoping in that time will change for the better.

You see nothing is going to change unless you want to work on changing it. You will often hear people say that the reason they got a divorce was because the love was gone. That's not true, because the love that you had for that person didn't leave you, you're the one left love.

Love didn't pack a bag and walk out of the door you did. Love did not walk out on you husband, wife, kids, boyfriend or girlfriend you did.

You see we asked for love we get love and then we turn around and leave love. We sometimes inflict physical, emotional, and mental abuse on the ones that we love. And the person that is taking the abuse doesn't know when enough is enough.

We are sometimes afraid to leave because we are not sure that we can make it on our own. We sometimes feel as if our lives would have know meaning if that person left us.

We allow ourselves to let other people dictate our happiness and put other people in control of our lives and emotions.

When they say jump, we don't ask why we just say how high. We ourselves become puppets allowing others to pull the strings, to control our every emotion. We some time even allow people to control our minds. We become institutionalized thinking that is the way it supposes to be. I don't care who you are it can happen to you. If it hasn't happened to you haven't ran into the right person yet, because it can happen to each and every one of us, if we allow it too.

Time is the only thing that will heal a broken heart. There is no wonder drug or magic potion to cure heartache, just time. We have to take back control of our minds, body and soul only then can we say enough is enough.

Everyone has options about love, this one happens to be MINE.
Freddie J. Moore

My Promise

I can't promise you forever
Because forever I'll never see
But I will love you one day at a time
And it will last eternity

I can't promise you the world
Because it's not mine to give
But I promise you from the depth of my soul
That your heart will be fulfilled

There are things that happen in our lives
That we cannot explain
There's no know explanation on how I feel
But I know it will never change

I loved you as a little boy
And into the man I've become
Because the moment I first saw your smile
I knew you were the one

My Love

Love is built with trust
One moment at a time
Honesty opens the door to our hearts
To explore our precious shrine

You have a heart of gold
You are a diamond in the rough
I can say these things to you everyday
And it still wouldn't be enough

I've waited a lifetime to say these things to you
But I was so insecure
Of you walking away in disbelief
It was my biggest fear

Now you know how I feel
And the things I've kept inside
When seeing you, I must admit
Is getting impossible to hide

Love Is

Love is something that we cannot touch
But possible to feel
Love is something we cannot hold
But possible to give

Love will often come to us
At any time of day
We can't see it but we kno
When it's gone away

We find ourselves looking for love
And we promise to protect
But love will find us when it's time
When we least expect

When loves decides to come your way
Keep an open heart
Because if it's true love we will know
And we will never fall apart

I Feel For You

Words cannot explain
The things I feel for you
Holding you close in my arms
I feel passion running through

Your passion flows like a river
Over beds of sparkling sand
Feeling your lips close to mine
Gives me the strength to stand

The things that makes us strong
Can also make us weak
The way I plan on loving you
Is a feeling I plan to keep

As I look into your eyes
I cannot help but stare
Imagining my body close to yours
Because I know I'll soon be there

My Heart to Yours

I would like to build a bridge
From my heart to yours
And have possession of the only key
That will open many doors

The door to your heart
Has been closed for awhile
Afraid to trust anyone,
This leaves you in self-denial

Taking a chance on love,
A hard choice to make
But if we take a chance together
That bond will be hard to break

I will give you the love
That your heart desires
And the strength I get from loving you
I know I'll never tire

Dreams of You

The feeling that I have for you
They will never change
I've tried so hard to suppress my thought
But they still remain the the same

I've always dreamed of loving you
Even as a child
To hold your hand and kiss your lips
I would walk a country mile

You often try to convince yourself
That I'm going through a stage
But if you would open the book to my heart
You would be on every page

When I look in your eyes
I could see being everything for you
So look in the mirror and ask yourself
If my feelings are really true

Open Your Heart

Opening up your heart
Is not an easy task
If my intentions were not honorable ones
I wouldn't even ask

Before you open a book
You wonder what's inside
I want you to open your heart to me
Because there I want to reside

You have the power
In many more ways than one
And the pain that's been caused in your life
Can never be undone

Making you forget your pain
Is not my intention
But we feel things deep in our souls
And we just have to listen

Finding Love

When I tell you the things I feel
You seem so afraid
You lock the door to your heart
And politely close the shade

Not wanting to take a chance
On a broken heart again
Because the hardest thing about finding love
Is losing it in the end

We often find ourselves
Afraid to take a chance
Remembering the song we listen to
And the way we use to dance

Those are the memories
That we wish would go away
But know matter how hard we try
In our heart they will always stay

My Heart Glows

A woman can possess a love
That will bring a man to his knees
And no matter how strong we are
We will put our heart on our sleeves

Being a man that falls in love
Is the strongest man I know
I have no problem in showing you things
That will make my heart glow

You might find it hard to believe
That a man would say these things
Thinking we have a one track mind
And just out for conquering

Some of us are, I must admit
We play a childish game
And this makes it even harder
For the ones that remain

Trusting

Trusting your heart to someone
Is a chance we choose to take
Sometimes we second guess ourselves
On the choices we sometimes make

We make the choice on who we love
And we pray it will be true
We can give someone our heart and soul
And not have it returned to us

If you are waiting on true love
That day may never come
But if you find true love you will know
Because it will be as warm as the sun

True love will keep you warm
On a cold winter's night
And will shine so bright in your eyes
In the early morning light

The List

Make a list of reasons
Why you should be with me
Then make another list
On why it should not be

The first list you make
Will be the longer one
Because I know we'll be together
After all is said and done

When I think that my emotions
Have gone as far as they can
I see the beauty in your eyes
And that makes me a stronger man

Breathing is my passion
That keeps you on my mind
Having the words to express my thoughts
Are never hard to find

To You

The day that I told you how I felt
To you was a big surprise
I know you could not help but think
Every time you close your eyes

I kept this inside for so long
It was beginning to take its toll
Pretending that you were my girlfriend
When I was eleven years old

We only live once
And I want that once with you
No matter the troubles the world may bring
I know we'll make it through

Trusting in each other
And being that best friend
We would be unbreakable
Unlike broken bones that mend

My Heart

If you had known my heart
I wonder how you would feel
Thinking it was a childhood crush
Or could it be for real

I know you have a lot on your mind
And you may be confused
You make me say things and write words
That I have never used

When it comes to you it's easy
To say what's in my heart
Because not telling you how I feel
Would not be very smart

Know matter what your friends say
Or the number of books you've read
I am here to tell you
That chivalry is not dead

You Will Never Be Alone

Don't be afraid to put me in your heart
Or of things you want to say
Trust in your mind, body and soul
That I will never go astray

You've probably heard things before
That caused you to lose your faith
I know in my heart the thing that I feel
And that I would never take

Sometimes we are by ourselves
A choice to be on our own
But as long as I have a beating heart
You will never be alone

We sometimes use our past
To dictate our future plan
Keeping us from things we desire
Or things we don't understand

You Touch My Soul

You feel as if you could love me
But you don't say the words
You touch my soul with you heart
And I feel the songs of humming birds

I can feel your presence
When we are far apart
I've waited so long to say what I thought
But didn't know where to start

Love is a feeling
That we could never change
No matter how hard we attempt to try
It will always remain the same

Every word that I write
Is what I feel inside
Take my hand, close your eyes
And let your heart open wide

Time After Time

I know that you've been loved before
Time after time
But if you put all of them together
It would not equal up to mine

My love for you is like an hourglass
Filled with grains of sand
The love I desire to give you
Will omit any other man

The words that I write
Is what I see in your eyes
You're like a caterpillar, you wait
For that love to turn into butterflies

I would give my last breath to save your life
Even if it meant losing mine
Because in my heart then I'll know
We will have a forever bind

My Desire

The things I feel for you
I've wondered if you wanted to know
I can't help but say what I feel
Because feelings continue to grow

My desire is to be with you
Every moment that I can
And not having to pick a day
Or just when we plan

I want the chance to hold you
And go deep in your mine
Because every time I touch you
It will feel like the very first time

I want to listen to your heartbeat
And know what's being said
Because I've been lost so many times before
But by your heart I'm being led

Love Makes Us

Love is not what we make it
Love makes us
And if we neglect its needs
It will surely turn to dust

I want to plant a seed in your heart
And nurture it with love
And when that seed begins to grow
It will be as high as the sky is above

Love will grow inside of your heart
Like it is a distant land
And not want to be touched
By any other man

You will know in your soul
That your love belongs to me
And all the years that pass us by
You will know we were meant to be

The Things I Feel

Telling you the things that I feel
Is not me being bold
I've been carrying it around for so long
Now it's time to lighten the load

Love is not a burden
Because my load is filled with care
The load I've carried all these years for you
Is a load I have loved to bare

If you could see the future
Would I be the one you choose?
The answer lies within your heart
And in my heart it grows

The answer that you are seeking
Is just beyond your reach
There are so many things I want to learn
But only you can teach

Things of the Heart

I want to be with you
But it's more than a physical thing
I can make you feel things of the heart
That a touch will never bring

You will feel me everyday
At any giving time
And if you're not holding me in your arms
You're holding me in your mind

There are so many emotions in my heart
That I can never explain
I can touch you everyday
And it would never be the same

Loving a woman such as yourself
I sometimes become afraid
Hoping that I don't repeat mistakes
That I've already made

My First Love

I want you to know
That you were my first love
To the depths of the sea
And to the heavens above

My promise to you
Is a dedicated will
To love you forever
Or for as long as I live

There is a secret to love
That everyone knows
Say I love you everyday
And that will make it grow

Where ever our love takes us
I will not be afraid
I will live happily ever after with you
And with the choice that I made

Being in Love with You

You are my life
And the air that I breathe
Loving you like no other man
Is the goal I plan to achieve

If you never believe
That true love exists
Take a look over your shoulder
And I will be in your mists

I will love you in three places
At the same time
And those three places are
Your heart, soul and mind

Being in love with you
Is not just a dream
Because the love for you in my heart
Keeps flowing like a stream

Forever More

Every time I see you
My heart fills with cheer
Because listening to your voice
Is like music to my ear

Sometimes I often let
My problems get me down
But hearing your voice everyday
Brings the sweetest of sounds

Sounds that I hear
I've never heard before
And sound that I would like to hear
Forever more

My promise is to love you
From dusk 'til dawn
And the passion I have inside for you
Keeps getting strong

Take My Hand

All I'm asking you to do
Is just take my hand
Because the love I'm going to plant
Will grow in desert sand

Trust will be the sun
Honesty will be the rain
And that will be the mystery
That love can only explain

I will love you everyday
And will always keep you warm
I will shelter you from the rain
And in a thunderstorm

There are going to be hard times
That will come our way
But if we stand hand and hand
There will be a brighter day

Dreams

When I look in your eyes
There are so many things I see
Making love to you in the moonlight
Is my biggest fantasy

Dreams are sometimes things
That are yet to come
The love I plan on giving you
Will never be undone

The kind of love that I plain to give
Lies deep within my mind
And I promise my love with all my heart
Until the end of time

My love is on a battlefield
Which happen to be your heart
I don't know how it will end
But from you, I will never part

Falling in Love

My intentions are to make you smile
In every way that I can
Catering to your every need
Or simply holding hands

If you only knew the joy you brought
When we are all alone
Staring in your eyes
Makes my heart strong

There are things that happen in our lives
Falling in love is just one
You make me want to love you
In ways that have never been done

I wanted so bad to say these things
But I didn't know where to start
You are the Mona Lisa to my soul
Which makes you a beautiful work of art

I'm sorry

I made mistakes in my life
That I cannot deny
No one is perfect in this world
But we still often try

There are things in our lives
That we have to learn
I can't promise you a perfect life
But you will be my first concern

I've always felt in some strange way
That we had a connection
I have to say my heart for you
Is filled with affection

You are like a rose in a garden
Because when it starts to bloom
I can sense your presence in the air
From across a room

Your Heartbeat

I am not that little boy
That you have known
And now that I've become a man
My feelings have also grown

When it comes to loving you
I am filled with greed
I have a desire for no one else
Because you are all I need

I want to hold you in my arms
And listen to your hear beat
And watch over you all night long
While you are asleep

When I look into your eyes
You sometimes look away
Afraid of things that you feel
Or what I was going to say

Love is Pure

Don't be afraid of loving me
Because I know your love is pure
As long as I know I'm in your heart
I have nothing in this world to fear

You are the last thought of my night
And the first thought when I awake
You are in every beat of my heart
And in every breath I take

My love for you is in my heart
Floating like a dove
And every time I look in your eyes
I could write a book of love

You have your heart locked in a cage
And you have the only key
And if you let me open the door
You would fall in love with me

Give Me a Chance

One of your concerns is
What people will say
If you believe I'm true to my word
You should not keep me away

I want to be the one
That you can trust
But some times I feel
That I'm not good enough

Making my feeling known to you
I feel I'm out of my league
My crime is wanting to love you
And guilty I will plead

We have heard all our lives
That love is blind
The love I plan on giving you
I promise is one of a kind

Loving You is Easy

Don't be afraid
Of the thing that you hear
Because my last intention
Is causing you to fear

I want to be in your life
And there I plan to stay
Because it really doesn't matter to me
What other people say

This is your decision
Because I have already made mine
And I know we have something
They will never find

Loving you is easy
I don't have to read a book
Because love is not hard to find
You just have to look

Your Lover, Your Friend

My dreams are to be your lover
As well as your best friend
And it will surely take us places
That we have never been

The moment I enter your body
Your tensions you will release
And I will hold your body close to mine
Until you fall asleep

For me it's more than a physical attraction
And more than the eyes can see
Because I have longed to feel the touch
Of your body lying next to me

My desires for you is like a furnace
That burns deep within
The passion will run through your body
And have sweat dripping from your skin

My Lover, My Friend

I know what I'm talking about
Because I've been there before
No matter how many times we made love
I wanted her even more

It was like an addiction
And she was my drug
Counting the times I wanted her
Are like counting the stars above

Just thinking about her
Got me through the day
I would lay down my life for her
If that's the price I had to pay

Sometimes people bring things out
That we don't know we have within
So open your heart to me
And be my lover and my friend

Ask Yourself

You will ask yourself
If I'm really true
Because no man can make you
Feel the way I do

You will want to please you
In any and every way
You will find yourself thinking about me
In the middle of the day

At night will be even worse
When you are trying to rest
Thinkin about how it would feel
With your head on my chest

You will try to control yourself
With all you might
Of waking me up to make love
In the middle of the night

Thoughts of Loving You

Not telling you how I feel
I would have nothing to gain
Because the thought of loving you
Is driving me insane

I would like to lay you gently
Face down on a mat
And kiss you from your neck
To the center of your back

Anticipating on touching you
And staring in your eyes
My body will lose control
As my body began to rise

Our temperature will rise
Leaving us out of control
And it will be the greatest love story
That's ever been told

The Passion

I want to make you feel things
That you have never felt
I want to put my hands in places
That makes your body melt

I will take you places
Only in your mind you will go
And the passions that you desire
Will make your juices flow

Your heart will give a beat
That makes my soldiers march
And as I enter foreign soil
My back will began to arch

I will take you places in your mind
That you have never been
And the love that I give you
You will pray it never ends

Your Eyes

When I look into your eyes
You long to feel my hand
I will touch you from head to toe
And start over again

Our bodies will be entwined
And being glad they met
Making love to the midnight
Until the sheets began to sweat

If I made love to you
I would be afraid to close my eyes
Thinking it's just a dream
Or something I fantasize

Trusting me with your body
Is something that you fear
Giving me the love you desire
And praying I don't disappear

Forever Yours

Walking out of your life
Is the last thing I would do
Because it took me so many years
To say these word to you

I don't know what you desire
But I know what I want to give
And the love I have in store for you
Is a love that you will always feel

I will be in your thoughts
At any giving time
And when you close your eyes at night
You will see me in your mind

You will ask yourself the question
If this man is really for me
Does he love me the way he says
Or is he like the other three.

Your Beauty

I have always thought you were beautiful
And that is plain to see
But if I cannot be in your heart
Your body means nothing to me

Sometimes we judge beauty
On what is in our eyes
But I judge your beauty
On what you feel inside

I can't stop these feeling
And I don't think I should
Because I've felt this way for awhile
And wouldn't stop them if I could

We don't want to see things
But our hearts are never deaf
Thinking we couldn't be more than friends
But you are only fooling yourself

Thinking of You

Sunshine often comes in our lives
And sometime the wind may blow
But we are also thankful for the rain
That makes the rose in your heart grow

There are so many things you can teach
And from me I want to learn
Because thinking about you everyday
Makes my heart yearn

Sometimes we miss what is sent to us
Waiting on a sign
I want to hold you close to me
With your eyes staring into mine

Every time we make love
It will never be the same
You will find yourself waking up at night
Calling out my name

It's Only Natural

Open up your heart
And let nature take its course
You will feel things you never felt
But it will never be remorse

You can climb the highest mountain
Or cross the deepest sea
And there I will be on the shore
Because you are my destiny

You often say a prayer
Seeking a godly man
Then you choose on your own
That which is not in God's plan

You will surely know
If you were meant for me
Because God will not show you things
That were not meant to be

A Man's Love

The thing I feel for you
I will never understand
And I know having these feelings
Is part of being a man

This is a feeling
We sometimes try to hide
Not wanting to show
Our sentimental side

When we show this side
We feel as if we are weak
And being in control of our emotions
Is something no one can teach

When I look in your eyes
I'm taught things I never knew
And every lesson that's being taught
I would run through fires for you

Your Inner Beauty

You have inner beauty
And you are filled with grace
And beside those words in a dictionary
Is a picture of your face

Words cannot explain
What you mean to me
Being the man that loves you forever
Is the man I want to be

Time will only tell
If my heart is true
But you can tell right now
If I'm the one for you

You can feel me in your heart
And you can feel me in your mind
But you are still sitting alone
Waiting on a sign

Teach Me

There is always bad weather
When gray clouds fill the skies
But what does it mean to you
When I'm starring in your eyes

There is one thing in this world
That we all should understand
It takes a good woman
To turn a boy into a man

Teach me to hold you in my arms
And be gentle as a dove
Tell me the things your heart desires
And teach me how you want to be loved

Loving you the way you should be
That is the plan
And if you were beside me every day
I would be a better man

My Greatest Vision

The feelings that I have for you
I kept them hidden inside
And now that they have come to life
I couldn't stop them if I tried

Letting you know how I felt
Was my decision
Now that you know how I feel
Makes you my greatest vision

I want us to experience things together
That we have never done
Like shinning so bright in each other's eyes
Just like the evening sun

It makes me feel good
Since you have come my way
There is only one problem that I have
Not having enough hours in the day

It's Real

Sometimes we make our decisions
On what's pleasing to the eyes
We're attracted to a pretty package
When we don't know what's inside

Lust last for a moment
When we give each other pleasure
But passion will last a lifetime
And that's what we should treasure

Sometimes we may find ourselves
Looking for a thrill
And when true love comes our way
We wonder if it's for real

Love can be counting stars at night
Or counting drops of rain
It is impossible to do
Because the number is never the same

Reason to Believe

Your eyes are filled with beauty
That I wish to possess
And when I see your beautiful smile
My heart beats through my chest

To have possession of an ounce of your love
Would be my greatest wealth
And I know if you gave it to me
I would take it to my death

I have always wanted you to know
What I'm all about
But every time I wanted to speak
The words would not come out

I'm asking for a chance
To give you a reason to believe
Because the feelings that I have inside
You will never be deceived

In My Heart

Telling you how I feel
Or simply holding you hand
I will give you the love your heart desires
And follow your every command

Can you imagine the feeling
Of being loved everyday
Waiting for one to end
And for the other to come into play

Your happiness is not for me to promise
It's what I desire to do
Because the things I feel inside my heart
Is like a river running through

Infidelity is not a feeling
It's a choice that we make
Loving you with my heart and soul
Is a vow I will never break

A Life Together

The emotions that you have
Make you question what you feel inside
And the things that hold you back
Is what's in your heart

I have waited so long
To say what you mean to me
I will climb the highest mountain for you
And swim the deepest sea

If with us it was meant to be
Time will only tell
But if our love is from the heart
It will never fail

We can build a life together
And it may even fall
But it's better to have love and lost
Than never have loved at all

Shower You With Love

You might ask yourself the question
Of why it has to be you
There is no question on how I feel
Or the things I want to do

Sometimes we are afraid
Of the answer we might get
We know the feelings in our hearts
But it's something we are afraid to admit

The things that are going through your mind
Leaves you confused
But if you put me in your heart
It's a place I would never use

I know you've had a broken heart
Which leaves you afraid to trust
Let me shower it with love
So it will never turn to dust

To Be Your Man

Sometimes we often feel
We can do without love
But we need it like the grass needs rain
That falls from the sky above

We think if we don't get it
It's something we'll never miss
Afraid to put that piece in your heart
And having it not fit

If we try and fail
That makes us want to cease
But sometimes making the wrong choice
Is worth finding the right piece
You are filled with beauty
And I want to be your man
Because the things I feel for you
You will never understand

Statue in My Heart

You are an elegant lady
Filled with confidence
And if there were anything that frighten you
I would come to your defense

You are a painter's masterpiece
As he uses the right tone
You are the statue in my heart
That was sculpted out of stone

I will love, honor, and cherish you
And all of me I would give
Because inside your beating heart
Is where I want to live

I would move out insecurity
And I would also move self-doubt
And replace it with the thing
That has been left out

My Plan

The way I plan on loving you
I could never count the ways
Because when I look into your eyes
I would get lost in a maze

Looking into your eyes
Are the windows to your soul
I want you to trust me with the secrets
That you have never told

Tell me the hurt
That's been left behind
And I will do all I can
To remove it from your mind

Tell me the pain
That's been in your heart
Because if its still there
I want to know where to start

Making Love to You

I want to touch you in places
That others could not find
And if you lost your sight tomorrow
You could see me in your mind

Wanting to make love to you
Is not just a physical thing
I would be emotionally paralyzed
From the touch you would bring

Holding you in my arms
And not wanting it to end
We could take each other places
That we have never been

The things that I've felt for you
I have felt all of my life
I wanted to tell you so many times before
But you were someone else's wife

Worth the Wait

I have longed for you
To feel my lips
Kissing you gently
While you strip

Sometimes I lay in bed
And I often fantasize
Of kissing you softly
On your inner thighs

A chill will cover your body
From my slightest touch
But it is a feeling
That you have wanted so much

I want you to trust me
And to me open your gate
Because when I enter your garden
It will be worth the wait

Sweetest Song

The things I have inside
Could never be so real
And if the shoes were on your feet
Could you tell me how you feel

Could you say these things to me
That I've waited to say for so long
Because hearing your voice everyday
Brings the sweetest song

When I look into your eyes
You don't have to say a word
Because the way my heart beats inside for you
Is a beat I never heard

If we were together would it be fate
Or something I wanted to be
But I can tell you from my heart
That you are my destiny

Trust Me

Trust me when I touch you
Because it will be with respect
And the ways you want to touch me back
Only you will select

Show me the things
That you want to express
And the pain that was left behind
You would think about even less

Sometimes we will wish
The past would disappear
But if we didn't go through bad times
We wouldn't know what to fear

I want to be with you
But that's my biggest fear of all
Because the things that I feel for you
Keeps flowing like a waterfall

Special Love

Have you ever wondered
How it would feel to be with me
Waking up beside each other
And I'm the first face that you see

How would that make you feel
As you asked the question why
Would you have the desire to be with me
As each day goes by

Would you be happy to see me
Each and everyday
Wondering if what you are feeling
Will ever go away

Life itself is one thing
That we will never understand
And finding that special love
Is not always in our plan

A New Love

You can tell a lot about a person
By looking at their smile
It's hard when it comes to you
Because you haven't done it in a while

Happiness is what you already have
It's not something someone gives
You have closed the door to your heart
And that's where your happiness lives

Not wanting to share it
Thinking it would be taken away
Protecting yourself from all others
And wanting your happiness to stay

You are afraid to be loved
Thinking it will someday end
Or afraid of a new love
That will take you where you have never been

Love is Blind

We have all of our lives
That love is blind
Not giving you the love you desire
That would be so unkind

The anticipation of pain
Is worse than pain itself
I will help you deal with the hurt
That the others left

Wanting you to love me
Is something you will do in time
You can search the world
And never find a love like mine

Now its time to close the book
On what you've just read
But it's going to stay on your mind
When you are alone in bed

Life is Love

How I plan to love you
I could never count the ways
But every time I saw your face
Would be a brighter day

Your ray of beauty
Will shine so bright
You will be my evening star
In the middle of the night

When the skies are not sunny
You will be my clouds filled with rain
Showering me with the love
That your heart will bring

Life is love
You take the good with the bad
That way we can find
Things that we never had

Trust in Me

I can make you feel things
That you never felt
And just like ice cream
In my arms you will melt

I will keep you warm
From a lonely chill
Because my desire for you
You will always feel

There are so many things
In my heart I feel
And I question myself
If they could be real

Trust in me
And the things I say to you
Because having you by my side
I know I will make it through

On My Mind

I look forward
To each day's end
Because I know
I will see beauty again

With you on my mind
The thoughts run so deep
That sometimes causes me
To talk in my sleep

You make me say things
With an unconscious mind
Things I have wanted to say
Time after time

I've wanted to hold your hands
And look into your eyes
And tell you all the things
That I've fantasized

Do you Think of Me

How many minutes of the day
Do you think of me
And when you close your eyes at night
What visions do you see

Are your dreams filled with things
We have never done
Because dreams are only testaments
Of things yet to come

I will climb the highest mountains
And swim the deepest sea
If that's what it takes to show
What you mean to me

The things that I feel for you
To you is a big surprise
Because I have longed to see
That sparkle in your eyes

Till the End

If I had the chance
To live my life over again
You are the only piece
I would want with me till the end

You made life better
With the love that you gave
You saw I was in troubled times
And me, you wanted to save

I put you through a lot
And these are things I can't change
And the day that you stop loving me
I will only have myself to blame

I have had a broken heart
Since the day you left
But now I'm asking for one more chance
To redeem myself

Love For a Year

I will take two months
To show you how I feel
Then it will take you three months
To know that I'm for real

I will take another two months
Spent on loving you
And I will take two more months
To show my love is true

One month will be spent
Showing the ways I love
And one month will be spent
Staring at the stars above

Another will be spent
Protecting you from fear
And just for the record
That's love for a year

Trust Me Again

I want to do the things for you
The things I failed to do in the past
It's not an easy task

Wondering if I will stand by
The things that you hear me say
Wondering if this feeling overtime
Will slowly pass away

Loving you in the way you deserve
In my heart I plan
And the kind of love that you gave
I don't want to lose again

The mistakes that I made
Is why we are apart
And I'm just asking once again
To let me touch your heart

Moments in My Life

There have been moments in my life
That I have chose
One is staring at you in the moonlight
As your body glows

Being with you a lifetime
Is what I would choose
Because the love that I have
I will never lose

Passion in your body
I know it often flows
As I fantasize the moments
Of taking off your clothes

The desire in my heart
Keeps flowing like a steam
Because making love to you is reality
And not just a dream

Second Chance

We rarely get a second chance
To rewrite our wrong
And every time we make mistakes
That day is forever gone

Unable to back the hands of time
Of the days in which we live
And wondering if the future will bring
A day that you will forgive

I can tell you that I'm sorry
Every single day
And still not have you come back to me
But it's the price I have to pay

I promised you my love forever
And to always put you first
And now the love you have for me is gone
But for it I will forever thirst

Without You

Sometimes I sit and wonder
How my life would change
Would I still be sitting alone
If you had not came

Would I be all alone
Walking through the park
Or would I be sitting alone
Way after dark

Would I be out there seeking love
Or wanting it to find me
Or would I be in the forest
Like a lonely tree

Those are the things I think about
When I'm staring in your eyes Because
I would be lost in this world
Without you by my side

Dreams of You

You changed my life
The day that we met
And I haven't stop feeling
These things yet

My heart was like clay
That you started to mold
Now you have me saying things
That I have never told

You have loved me in many ways
That has never been said
You have brought back to life
Things that I thought were dead

I have dreams about you at night
When I am asleep
When I awaken in the morning
It still leaves me weak

Touch From You

I always think of you
When I feel the wind blow
And no matter what direction it leads
I will not hesitate to go

I can't see it
When it touches my skin
Because it's like a touch from you
That I feel deep within

Real love is felt
Deep in the soul
And the love I have for you
Will never grow old

I am not a perfect man
And I might cause you pain
But the love I have inside for you
Will always remain

I Love You

Saying I love you everyday
I feel is not enough
Because every moment we are apart
I long to feel your touch

I want to love
Your mind, body and soul
And as a young man in life
I will do until I'm old

The love I have to give
I will never tire
Because having someone to love you like me
Is something that you desire

You are my hourglass
That is filled with sand
Our love will keep growing strong
And will not perish in a desert land

Hands of Time

There are days I often wish
I could turn back the hands of time
Having a chance to love you with the passion
That's in my heart and in your mind

Neglecting the time we are giving
Is a mistake we will always regret
We are giving time to do these things
But how soon will we forget

The times I spend with you
Leaves me wanting more
Because it took you time to trust me
To open up your door

Wherever our love takes us
And no matter where it goes
I promise you with all my heart
That is a door I will never close

Chance on Love

Let's take a chance on love
To see what it will bring
Will it smell like roses
Or will it flow like a stream

Are your hands filled
With a gentle touch
Because filling your body close to mine
I will never get enough

Anticipation of my touch
Is more intense than the touch itself
Because the kind of touch I desire to give
Is a touch you never felt

When you close your eyes at night
You will have thoughts of many things
And someday you will realize
That it was more than just a dream

Caring Ways

Since you have been in my life
I can't imagine being alone
The emptiness that I felt inside
Now it's all but gone

I only have you to thank
For your caring way
And since you've come in my life
Also comes brighter days

You make me want to do things in life
That I was afraid to do
Now I have the courage to do those things
And it's all because of you

Thank you for my laughter
And for my smile
Because those are just two things
That I haven't done in a while

What's Love

Love is passion
That we often fear
And it can also be words
That we sometimes hear

The meaning of the word
We may never find
Because we have all heard
That love is blind

I want to make love to your body
When I'm touching your mind
And you will feel the bond that we have
That you have never been able to find

Every time we are together
It will never be the same
And every time that I walk by
Your body will be calling out my name

Together

Not having you in my life
I would be settling for less
Because all of my deepest desires
To you I would confess

Telling you the things
That I'm afraid to share
Thinking that one day
That you wouldn't be there

I have kept things in my heart
And also in my mind
Knowing I would share with someone
At the right time

That time is right now
My vision is so clear
And as long as we are together
I have nothing in this world to fear

Time to Grow

I am not the same person
You met so long ago
And since we've been apart
I was given the time to grow

There are things that are in our lives
That are so important to learn
And the most important person in our lives
Should be our first concern

I have only myself to blame
For being all alone
But if you gave me one more chance
I will show you how I've grown

A broken heart is the only thing
That will never make a sound
I see the pain I caused in your eyes
Because there it is found

The pain that I caused
Will you please forgive
Because there is only room for one in my heart
And there you will always live

Give Me a Chance

Give me a chance
To make you believe
Because loving you is something
I never want to leave

Give me a chance
To look into your eyes
To let you know
There will never be goodbyes.

Will You Forgive

There are so many things
That I wish I had said
And now I am afraid
Of what lays ahead

Not showing the love
And it's you that I lost
Now I am the one
That's paying the cost

But it is debt
That will never be paid
Unless you forgive me
For the mistake I made

Right now it is something
That you cannot do
Because your heart
Is still broken in two

I Miss You

There have been times in my life
That I've been alone
Not missing that person
Until they are gone

Then we try and cherish
The moments that we had
But it doesn't stop the heart
From feeling so sad

I wonder how much more
My heart can endure
And I can search the world over
To never find a cure

We have all heard people say
That love is blind
But getting over a broken heart
Will only heal in time

You Are

You are my sunshine
After the rain
You are my healing
After the pain

You are my light
That shines so bright
You are my comfort
In the middle of the night

You are might strength
I need to stand
You are my water
In a desert land

You are my passion
That keeps me warm
You are my shelter
In the thunderstorm

There is nothing in this world
I would hesitate to do
Because my life would have no meaning
If I didn't have you

I'm just a man
Looking for love
And I've searched the skies
And mountains above

Maybe finding love
Wasn't meant for me
But I'm going to keep on looking
Until eternity

I Will Never Tire

I've longed to feel your touch
Because it's soft, gentle and kind
You make me feel things in my heart
That I thought I would never find

I want to be in your heart
Mind, body, and soul
Starting as a young man
I will love until I'm old

The love that I wish to give
I will never tire
Because every time I look in your eyes
I'm filled with desire

You are my hourglass
Trust and take my hand
And I will fill your heart with the love
As if I were desert sand

You're on my mind

Why can't I just
Get you off of my mind
I have tried to forget you
So many times

Sometimes I feel like
I'm in a pit of quicksand
And I wouldn't wish these feelings
On any other man

Everywhere I go
There's a man with his family
And a thousand times
I wish That man was me

Seeing couples together
I feel so sad
Because I know I lost the best thing
That I ever had

A Broken Heart

I sit in a dark room
With closed shades
Focusing on all
The mistakes that I made

Wondering if there's any
Thing that I could do
To change your heart
And let me come back to you

I'm asking you to forget
All the things that I've done
I'm asking for another chance
To correct some

The last thing that I want
Is for us to be apart
Because the dark room I mentioned
Happens to be my heart

Imagination

I lay in bed at night
Staring at the ceiling
And if your head were on my chest
How would I be feeling

Now I can only imagine
The things I would feel
Because the things I feel for you
Never felt so real

There are so many places
In this world I could go
But I would still smell your scent
Every time the wind blows

I want to hold you close to me
Staring into your eyes
Because they tell me things
Only I can recognize

My Choice

I would like for you to know
That you are my only choice
And sometimes when I call you at night
It's just to hear your voice

When you are talking to me
I hear the sweetest sound
And every word that you say
To my heart they're bound

Hearing you whisper softly in my ear
I know I'll never tire
Feeling your lips close to me
I will always desire

I want you to tell me things
That I have never heard
I want to know what you are saying
When you don't say a word

A Love Like Mine

I wanted to tell you so many things
But I waited for the right time
And if you searched the world over
You will never find a love like mine

I would hold you in my arms forever
And never let you go
And plant a seed in your heart
To watch the love grow

The things that I say to you
Are things you should hear
But knowing what I say is true
Causes you to fear

Sometimes making promises
Are easier said than done
But the way that I've felt all these years
You have to be the one

Within You

Maybe it's time
For me to say these things
My eyes are open
And I know it's not a dream

I've waited so long
To say what's in my heart
The only problem that I had
Was that I didn't know when to start

Knowing there is beauty within you
Is where I wan to be
And if you only took my hand
You would also see

Everyday you are on my mind
And only for you I would wait
Because the feeling that I have for you
No one could ever take

Listen to Your Heart

Staring from the windows
Of my heart and soul
Neither have eyes to see
But ready to explode

Feelings that I have for you
Are as deep as an ocean bed
Your heart has ears to hear
Things that have never been said

It's so easy to write these words
About things that I cannot touch
Even thou I can't see these things
I want them just as much

Listening to your heartbeat
Would also put mine at ease
And receiving the love you are willing to give
Is all we will ever need

Living Without You

Living without you
I haven't been the same
Because you are always on my mind
As the seasons change

Thinking about things
That I will always regret
And feeling this emptiness in my heart
That hasn't been filled yet

I've been in love with you,
Carrying feelings as a youth
But I didn't have the courage
To tell you the truth

When I am home alone
There are nights I cannot sleep
Remembering all the promises I made
And the ones I did not keep
To love, honor and obey your heart
But I neglected your feelings from the start

Broken Heart

A broken heart is the only thing
That will never make a sound
I see the pain that I caused in your eyes
And there it is found

The pain that was caused in your life,
Will you ever forgive?
Because there is room for only one in my heart
And you will forever live

I Remember

I remember us holding hands
And walking through the park
And remember making love
From dawn to dark

Rubbing your feet at night
Until you fell asleep
Now those are the memories
That I cherish so deep

Anyone that's been in love
Has a story to tell
About the ones that are in their heart
Where they will always dwell

Because after everything
Is said and done
We will then realize
That they were the one

I Wonder

Sometimes I sit and wonder
How my life would change
Would I still be sitting alone
If you had not came

Would I be all alone
Walking through the park
Or would I be sitting alone
Way after dark

Would I be out there seeking love
Or wanting it to find me
Or would I be in the forest
Like a lonely tree

Those are the things I think about
When I'm staring in your eyes
Because I would be lost in the world
Without you by my side

My Lover

The love I have for you
It will never change
You have touched me in so many ways
That I will never be the same

You've taken me on a journey
In which I have never been
And the things that I feel inside
I wish would never end

You are my lover
As well as my love
You were sent to me
From the skies above

You are my angel
And there is nothing I wouldn't do
Because I have spent my entire life
Looking for someone like you

Outside Looking In

I would see you around town
Hanging with your friends
And I never thought I would be
Outside looking in

Seeing you at a distance
In your own little world
As if I'm a deep sea diver
Still searching for my pearl

You are the kind of lady
That turned this boy into a man
And I wonder if I will ever
Get that chance again

To make you feel the things
That you felt before
Because in my heart for you
There is an open door

A Lonely Man

I wake up every morning
And wish a thousand times
That I could make it through the day
Without you on my mind

Looking in the mirror
I see a lonely man
That took you for granted
In ways I can't understand

Everyday that I come home
I'm checking for your calls
My answering machine is empty
That leaves me staring at the walls

The hardest thing about living
Is being all alone
Because when I held you close to me
I could feel the love was gone

There were several times
You wanted to be with your friends
That's when my conscience started telling me,
Man it's coming to an end

I tried so very hard
To correct my every wrong
But there was nothing I could do
Because the love was gone

Love is like the sun and the rain
You brighten my life and shower away the pain.
There is one thing that we should know,is that we need them both
If we want to grow.

My Mistake

It's another New Year's Eve
And I find myself alone
Looking back over my life
To try and find the wrong

Was there anything different
That I could have done
Because I know mistakes were made
And now I can't change the outcome

Now it is time
That we both move on
Because it is always darkest
Just before the dawn

I hope you find the thing in life
That I did not give
Because the feelings that are in my heart for you
Will forever live

The Love is Gone

Every time I look in your eyes
I see the love is gone
I've come to the end of the road
Now it's time to move on

Being with me wasn't easy
It's time to do what I have to do
And the forgiveness that I'm seeking
Can only come from you

Walking away from you
I admit that it's hard
But if you can't find it
In your heart to forgive
That's between you and God.

The hurt that I caused in your life
I can never undo
Because the pain I caused in your life
I feel it too

My name is Freddie Moore I was 42 years old when I started writing this. I am a father of three. I have a daughter, Ashley, and two sons, Donavan and Cameron, and let me add by three different women. I was only married once and that was to Cameron's mother which we have since divorced. With my mother and father was a family of seven children. On my father's side including all the children there are about thirteen of us. When papa got around he really got around. He has thirteen children by four different women that we know of. I grew up in the era that it was something that was accepted by some wives, having a woman at home and one in the streets. My mother knew just like the others, but she accepted the fact that a man was going to be a man, as long as they took care of home. All my father's children are close to one another and we all get along. You would think that we would have a problem with each other but we don't, we look at it like that his situation and we didn't have anything to do with it. So when he died we all came together for the first time in our lives, not that we didn't want to but we could never find the time, and the strange thing about life is that death has a way of bringing families together. If you think about it, you will find more people at a funeral than you will at birth. All of my father's children were there except three, John Thomas Moore Jr., Guy Moore, and Tracy Cohen, which were all incarcerated at the time of his death.

My older brother Alfred and I were joking about our father's obituary, saying that with all the different last names of his children people are going to have a hard time trying to figure out who the mothers are. My father was a very intelligent man. He knew World history, Black history, Economics, and World events.

I can remember when we had to bring our report cards home, back then we had Negro history as a subject and I got a "D" in that subject. My dad went through the roof and he said, "How can a black man get a "D" in Negro history and was born in Negro history?" And as far as the Bible goes, he wasn't a very religious man, my entire life I had never seen him read the Bible but he could tell you anything you wanted to know from Genesis to Revelations. And the only prayer I can remembering him asking God is that he didn't want to outlive any of his children. He asked God not to let him have to bury any of his children. With my older brothers there were times when my father thought he would have to but God heard is prayer. He tried teaching us things that would help us later in life. We were taught to have a good work ethic.

Growing up on our grandparent's farm we had to learn how to work, because my grandfather didn't play. When he said he wanted the field plowed by the end of the day he meant it. Even today I appreciate the things that my father taught me. And one of the things he always said to us was try not to be like him. His words were, "You might be as good as me, but you will never be better than I am." I guess we meant that no matter how high we go, we will always look up to him. Well that's enough about that. Let's talk about the reasons you are reading some of my writings. It is a fact at a woman needs to know that she is being loved. But some of us men feel as if it is not that important to us, as it is to them. What we do know about love? What have we been taught about love? What do we teach each other about love? The most important question of all is what is love? We have all heard the song by Al Green titled "Love and Happiness" something that will make you do wrong or make you do right. It will make you come home early or make you stay out all night. One of the biggest mistakes that we make is that we try to change how love is supposed to be. We fail to realize that we can't change something that was here before we were born, and it will be here long after we are gone. It's like when you bake a cake, if you follow the instructions that are written on the box it will come out the way that it is supposed to. But if we decide to add a little more sugar, maybe a couple more eggs, it will turn out better, but I won't. Love is similar to that; we sometimes try to find new things in a person to love thinking we will make it better. But if we cultivated the things that made us fall in love with that person in the beginning, that will be everlasting love.

There will never be another first kiss, but we can always remember how that first kiss felt. My definition of love is having a desire to be with that person every minute of each day, and every time that person touches you, it feels like you are being touched by them for the very first time. To me love is being willing to give that person your last breath to save their life, even if it meant losing yours. Love is hearing a person heart beat and knowing what they are saying without them ever saying a word. Love is a thought that makes us think and feel the things that we do. Everyone wants to know the secret of everlasting love, sorry there isn't one. We ourselves are that secret and it lies within each and every one of us. There are so many secrets in the world, but everlasting love is not one of them. Some of us men try to hold on to our women by using the wrong methods. Instead of showing them love and affection, we use jealousy, verbal abuse, physical abuse and threats of violence to make our ladies stay with us. It is a fact that a bee will stay with honey rather than vinegar. We men have to be that honey. But we are the ones that are afraid of being alone. Let's face it the first person that we had a bond with was a woman. She took care of us she bathed us, clothed us, fed us, and taught some of us how to be men. We were dependent on you as a child and we are sometime dependent on you as adults. We all know the saying it takes a good woman to make a good man, and fellows that's what we need. My opinion is that love allows us to change our ways and not allow us to change the mistakes we made, it allows us to change but does not allow us to change the things that we have already done. Love allows us passion and over time it will allow that passion to increase. Love allows us to love but does not allow love ones forever. Time gives us love for many things, but time will not give us love if we are not willing to give it back.

Every man that's been in. love has a story about love. This one happens to be mine. I've been in a relationship where I've lied and cheated on women, and it's not something that I am proud of. Some of us often use that phrase "I'm just a man" it's not that we are no good men, we just make no good choices, and try to justify it by using that phrase as if it is a get out of jail free card. Sometimes women often use it as well saying things like "girl you know how those men are" Sometimes we do things thinking we have gotten away. But sooner or later it will come back to bite us in the ass. You have a choice to give-out a good karma or a bad karma. Whichever it is, you will get it back three times more. Sometimes we try to hide how we feel about being in love. I will bet you that if you had a room that had fifteen women and fifty men, and you asked everyone to stand that's been in love or suffered a broken heart. You will still see more women stand than men. Why? Because some of us have too much pride to admit it, which sometimes leaves us to think we are the stuff. Thinking by having so many women keeps us from getting hurt, moving from one woman to the next. The first lady that I had feelings for wasn't love. I just had a big crush on her since I was about ten or eleven, but we will get to her later.

My first love was unexpected and sometimes those are the best relationships. We are no longer together, but to this day I believe that fate had a lot to do with us meeting. The story began with my cousin we both attended the same high school. Not only were we cousins, we were best friends. If you saw one of us you saw the other. It could have been a Tuesday night basketball game or a Friday night football game, we were there. I remembered he would pick me up in his beat up pinto that he had. He would keep a brick or even a car battery behind his seat just to keep it from sliding all the way to the back seat. He thought his car was the sharpest thing on the road, and I just let him kept thinking it.

One thing that I can say is that it got us from point A to point B. We were at school one day and I asked him if he had any single cousins on his father's side of the family. He said yeah I got a few, but let me get back to you tomorrow. So the next day at school he said cuz I talked to one of my cousins and she wants to meet you. Here is her number so give her a call. So later that night I called her, told her who I was, we talked for a while she told me a little about herself and I as well. I told her that I would like to meet her. It just so happens that my school was playing a basketball game at her school Friday night. I could not wait until Friday because we talked every night. I would tell my cousin every day I got to school. I would say, "Hey man I talked to your cousin last night." The only problem I had is that I didn't know what she looked like. He told her that I would be with him so she would know was.

Friday finally got there, he picked me up as usual. As we were walking in I told him to point her out as soon as he saw her. All night long I would ask is she here yet, is she here yet? He would say no not yet. I was beginning to get mad because I was thinking she stood me up. So during halftime, we stood in the lobby for the rest of the game. While we were standing there this girl walked up and to my cousin and started talking to him. I asked him if that was her, he said no. He said she goes to school with his sister and was asking him about her. I'm still waiting on his cousin to show up. But every time I turned around this girl was still pulling on my cousin. I would say what did she want this time? His reply was she didn't want anything, but she stayed in his face the rest of the night. The game ended and we were still standing in the lobby. He turned to me and said cuz I guess she decided not to show up. I admit

I was a little disappointed after waiting all week. After the game was over we were still standing there talking, and out of nowhere this young lady walked up to me and said, "Hi, I just wanted to say bye," and she walked away without saying her name or anything else. I turned to my cousin and asked if that was her. He said no that's my other cousin. I said, "Are you lying to me?" He said, "Really, that's my cousin." I told him to forget your other cousin, because that's the one I want. By that time this guy walked up and started talking to my cousin.

When he left I asked, "Who was that?" He said, "That was her brother, and he doesn't like it when guys try to talk to his younger sister." I told him, "That's ass whipping I'm going to have to take because you are going to tell her that I would like to call her." This woman stayed on my mind all night long. I didn't sleep at all that night. Every time I closed my eyes I would see her face. I would hear those words, "Hi I just wanted to say bye" over and over again. The next day I asked him about the cousin that I was supposed to meet. He said, "Cuz she was there." I said, "Really?" He said, "That girl that kept pulling on me was her, but she told me not to tell you who she was." You better believe I had a few choice words for him. I told him he did me a favor because that was not the one I wanted to meet. But he still would not help me out. For months and months Iasked. So I told him with or without his help I was going to get to know her. So one night I was walking through the mall, and saw her from a distance. And I could not believe how nervous I was. I know that it was in the month of December because she had packages in her hands. To this day I cannot remember what we talked about or what I said to her, we talked for a few seconds and then her older sister walked up. She said, "This is my sister."

When she walked away I said to myself, I should've asked for her number. I was thinking I would never see her again. For the second time I let her slip through my fingers. A few months had passed, the next time talked I can remember it like it was yesterday. I was home watching the movie Jaws. The phone rings and my sister told me it's for me. I wondered who it could be calling me. I said, "Hello?" And this person said, "Hi, this is Mike's cousin." I said, "Who?" She said, "Mike's cousin." I could not believe what I was hearing, after all this time we are finally getting a chance to talk. I'm telling you we talked on the phone that night for about three hours about everything under the sun.

And that conversation led into a five year relationship. She was the first person that showed me what love was, and how it felt to be loved. That is the thing that I most appreciated about her. I can truly say she was my first love. After we split I didn't think I would love another person that deep again. That was until I met my wife, well ex-wife now. We started out as friends, as we got to know each other our feelings changed. We fell in love, got married and had a beautiful son together. But sometimes we don't appreciate what we have until it's gone. We should always put our first and second to no one. That is a mistake that I made and I will regret it for the rest of my life. She didn't ask for much. The only thing that she wanted was for me to love her, which I neglected to do so. That is one reason I'm writing this now, hopefully someone else won't make the same mistakes I made.

If I could do it over there are a lot of things I would do different. Now to the first lady that I didn't love but had feelings for. Like I said earlier I was about ten or eleven years old when I first saw her. She lived right down the road from where I lived. It was her father, mother, and younger brother and sister. The first time that I saw her, my older brother and I were playing with her brother behind their trailer. She and her younger sister were looking out of the back window. That's when I saw her, it was like a feeling I had never felt before. And as I grew older so did the feelings that I had for her, right along with her beauty.

It was like God himself had her put together with pacific directions.

Her eyes, her nose, her lips an so on, to me she was perfect in every way.

I finally made up my mind that I would tell her how I feel. After thirty-one years I told her, she could not believe it. She had no idea that I felt this way about her for all these years. I really think it was something she needed to hear. For a man to tell a woman how he feels for her is something hard to do.

We sometimes have trouble finding the words or maybe we want to say it, but our pride sometimes gets in the way. But, gentlemen forget pride, when it comes to your lady telling her how you feel is not you being weak. All our lives we were led to believe that men aren't suppose to cry.

That's a lie, we were taught as a child. That's one reason there are so, many divorces today, because of our stupid pride. So, gentlemen after you read this I'm sure you will find something to say to your lady.

Or ladies there might be something you can say to your man.

A while back a friend of mine asked me what I liked most about being married, I said having someone to come home to everyday and to share things with.

I said waking up in the middle of the night and seeing that person lying next to you.

Telling her how much she means to you with a look or a touch.

That's what I miss the most about being married.

So, men and women after you've read this maybe it will be something you won't have to miss.

www.ingramcontent.com/pod-product-compliance
Lightning Source LLC
Chambersburg PA
CBHW072036110526
44592CB00012B/1442